GROUND-BREAKING FASHION

Jane Rocca

Illustrations by Juliet Sulejmani

CONTENTS

INTRO-
DUCTION

Featuring punk icons, pop stars and fashion trail blazers, Groundbreaking Fashion reveals the most iconic looks and fashion game-changers of the past century.

There are 100 extravagant moments here drawn from every corner of fashion: from the scandalously short miniskirts of the Swinging Sixties to Diane von Fürstenberg's form-flattering wrap dress in the '70s; from Debbie Harry's post-punk repurposing of a plastic garbage bag as a coat in Blondie's 'Atomic' video clip to the meat dress Lady Gaga wore to the 2010 MTV Awards; and from fashion's best accessories and innovations to flamboyant fashion designers past and present. We worship these hall-of-fame moments and celebrate all that is unique about their contribution to fashion.

From Christian Dior's post–World War II 'The New Look' collection to the feminine power suit of the '80s, fashion has always been inspired by cultural and political movements, and is at the forefront of change. But fashion is also a product of its time, which we can see through the new wave influence in Vivienne Westwood and Malcolm McLaren's Pirate Collection in 1981, in the grunge-meets-fashion grit of Anna Sui's 1993 collection, and in the feminist statement coats Prada sent down the runway in 2014. Groundbreaking Fashion explores the essence of these, the biggest moments in fashion, and how they shaped generations.

We're not an A to Z guide, but rather, a salutation to the fashion looks that were a stitch ahead of their times, and a handy go-to catalogue of the moments that still inform our fashion today.

Jane Rocca

100 ICONIC MOMENTS

FROCK 'N' ROLL

BJÖRK IN MARJAN PEJOSKI'S SWAN DRESS

When Icelandic songstress Björk turned up to the 2001 Academy Awards wearing a swan dress by Macedonian designer Marjan Pejoski, it ruffled more than a few red carpet feathers (particularly when the kooky singer pretended to lay eggs on the red carpet as she made her grand entrance). Pejoski had created the dress for his 2001 Fall/Winter runway collection before Björk chose to wear it on the red carpet. He was inspired by the motion of animals and merry-go-rounds, and used the swan to capture movement and flight at once. It was a radical intersection of art and fashion – and while Björk's appearance at the Oscars was described as a 'miss' on the red carpet at the time, the white wrap-around frock was included in the Museum of Modern Art's retrospective exhibition on Björk's work in New York in 2015. It was a fitting dress for Björk, who as an eclectic performer is known to push boundaries with her music as much as her fashion ensembles. The flighty piece is now regarded as an iconic moment in fashion, shifting from fashion disaster to epitome of kooky cool in less than 20 years. What's more, Valentino designers Maria Grazia Chiuri and Pier Paolo Piccioli reimagined the dress as part of their couture show at Paris Fashion Week in 2014.

2001

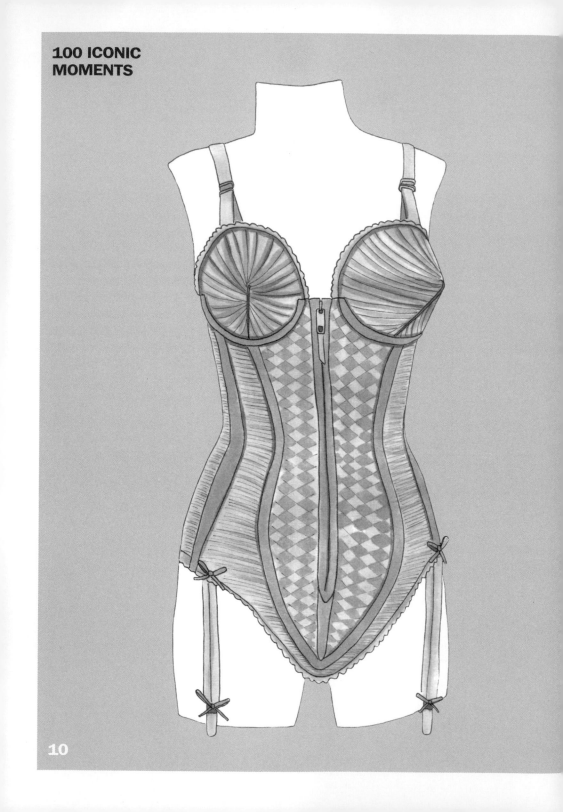

MADONNA IN JEAN PAUL GAULTIER'S CONE BRA

Madonna's iconic cone brassiere was designed by French fashion designer Jean Paul Gaultier, who debuted the style in his 1983 runway collection. The singer first wore the cone bra in her 1990 Blond Ambition tour. The infamous piece of lingerie was inspired by '50s bullet bras and '80s corsetry. Madonna combined Catholic religious iconography with her sensual bedroom eyes and this saucy number, giving pop a major fashion moment. The look was risqué for its time – if merely for the way Madonna got people thinking about religion and forbidden sexual desire. This is when underwear became outerwear, when cleavage and corsetry lived in harmony and Madonna was the key figure in bringing the message home. Gaultier and Madonna forged a friendship that saw the pair continue to collaborate after the Blond Ambition tour, and one of the cone bras eventually sold at a Christie's auction for US$52,000.

1990

LADY GAGA IN FRANC FERNANDEZ'S MEAT DRESS

When Lady Gaga turned up to the 2010 MTV Music Video Awards wearing a dress made of raw meat, it made fashion history. The dress was designed by Franc Fernandez and styled by now creative director of Diesel, Nicola Formichetti. Gaga's mother famously asked Formichetti what her daughter would be wearing on the night and he cheekily replied, 'it's in the fridge'. Gaga didn't anticipate the backlash by PETA activists against the dress, but she claims it wasn't supposed to offend vegetarians. The political message tied to the dress stems from Gaga's stance on the US government's don't-ask-don't-tell military policy; she was urging the US not to discriminate against gay and lesbian men and women who wanted to serve in the army. The vegan pop star said in an interview that the dress was meant to demonstrate that if we don't stand up for the issues we believe in, then we'll end up with as many rights as meat. The dress was displayed in the Rock and Roll Hall of Fame in 2011, who paid taxidermist Sergio Vigilato US$6,000 dollars to preserve the dress.

2010

KYLIE MINOGUE'S GOLD HOTPANTS

The year was 2000 and Kylie Minogue's bottom-hugging gold hotpants in the 'Spinning Around' video clip made all eyes turn towards her rear and put her album *Light Years* on high rotation in Australia and the UK. According to Minogue, the hotpants were purchased by a friend for 50 pence at Kensington market in London, and she first wore them at a Nerds, Tarts and Tourists themed party. Her good friend, creative director and stylist William Blake, spotted them in her wardrobe and decided they'd be perfect for the 'Spinning Around' clip. The pants referenced the disco pulse of the '70s, when hotpants were seen on fashionable bottoms in dance clubs everywhere, and allowed the Australian pop princess to shift her image from pop artist to disco diva.

2000

KANYE WEST AND ADIDAS YEEZY SNEAKERS

Being a step ahead in fashion means you're winning when you're working with others – collaborating in the name of more fame. Let it be known that collaborations are lucrative, collectible and usually work best when the talent is a huge name with an astronomical social media following. Enter Kanye West, who started collaborating with Adidas in February 2015 for what *The New York Times* said was a US$10 million price tag. His famous Yeezy Boosts, sneakers that have seen his fans queue up for days in various cities around the world when released, might have entered the market at US$350 but they're so sought after that at last check, eBay was asking US$1400. The Grammy Award–winning rapper has also worked on a sportswear range with the giant retailer in a bid to merge his music identity with fashion and lifestyle. Ever since Kanye's hugely popular collaboration, many other celebrities have joined their star power with brands in collabs, like Rihanna with Puma, Gigi Hadid with Stuart Weitzmen and Idris Elba with Superdry.

2015

DEBBIE HARRY IN BLONDIE'S 'ATOMIC' VIDEO CLIP

When Blondie's frontwoman Debbie Harry wore a plastic garbage bag as a jacket in their 1979 video clip for 'Atomic' – a single from their *Eat to the Beat* album – it was a comment on the future of New York and pop culture. At the time the city streets were exploding with rubbish, prompting Harry to don her garbage bag as an ode to a city on the brink of stink. The platinum blonde was also wearing a Vultures t-shirt, which she found in a thrift store and wore endlessly, including in a notable moment captured on camera backstage at the Whisky a Go Go in 1978. Even though the look gave us New York post-punk cool with a nod to disco, Harry never considered herself a style icon – she was merely recycling, finding clothes at second-hand stores and being guided by her late friend and stylist Stephen Sprouse, who lived in the same building as she did.

1979

RIHANNA IN GUO PEI AT THE 2015 MET GALA

When Rihanna rocked up to the Met Gala in 2015 wearing a magnificent gold couture gown by Chinese designer Guo Pei it took everybody's breath away and became the most talked-about outfit at the event. The imperial yellow fox fur–trimmed cape, embroidered with flora scroll patterns, weighed over 25 kilograms (55 pounds) and took Pei 50,000 hours over 20 months to make by hand. A pink mini-dress was fitted underneath. Pei originally debuted the coat on the runway in 2010. The theme for the 2015 Met Gala was 'China: Through the Looking Glass'. Rihanna found Pei via a Google search and contacted her about wearing the cape, although Pei initially didn't know who Rihanna was. It's a merging of worlds made in couture heaven, where Chinese traditional costume is woven into a ballgown fit for a queen – or a pop princess in this case.

2015

CYNDI LAUPER IN THE 'GIRLS JUST WANNA HAVE FUN' VIDEO CLIP

The '80s, a time when rah-rah skirts, teased hairdos and chewing gum were the norm, belonged to Cyndi Lauper – the queen of radio pop and rebellious girl cool. Lauper worked closely with stylist Patrick Lucas in her heyday and he was responsible for Lauper's style in the 'Girls Just Wanna Have Fun' video clip. The clip saw Lauper wearing a range of classic '80s outfits including a red bustier and a giant crinoline skirt, and a pink vintage taffeta dress with a stole. She led the brigade of girls just wanting to have fun with fashion, mixing together all sorts of different '80s styles. The iconic track became an anthem for the decade and inspired girls around the world to embrace fingerless gloves, pointy lace-up style booties, giant earrings and punk-inspired hairdos.

1983

THE BAND T-SHIRT

It wasn't until the 1960s that band t-shirts became a phenomenon; thanks to acts such as Elvis Presley, The Monkees and The Beatles, wearing merchandise like the band tee pledged allegiance to a group. Fans liked nothing more than showing their support of a rock 'n' roll or pop act by wearing the band's name on a t-shirt. By the time the '70s rolled around, glam, metal and punk acts embraced the band t-shirt and it has since become a staple in any music lover's wardrobe. Original t-shirts are now highly collectable. Bands know the value of merchandise and always produce a new print when releasing an album. But it's not just the rock 'n' rollers who have held onto the rebelliousness of a band t-shirt – international runway shows and social media stars have all embraced the cool that is the band tee.

1960s

AMY WINEHOUSE'S RETRO STYLE

Amy Winehouse, who died in 2011 at the age of 27, was a British singer and songwriter who fused the best of female jazz with a dose of '60s girl cool. With a sky-high beehive hairstyle and heavy black eyeliner, Winehouse became a poster girl for revivalist soul. She was pin-up perfection in her healthier days, and inspired a generation of young women to wear an up-do. It was never about the fashion for Winehouse though, as her artistry lay in her songwriting. She penned some of her most famous songs, including 'Back to Black' and 'Rehab', about drugs and losing love. She was retro, had a hankering for old-school tattoos and wore her heart on her sleeve. French couture designer Jean Paul Gaultier paid a tribute to the star in his 2012 Spring Couture show.

2011

MICHAEL JACKSON IN THE 'THRILLER' VIDEO CLIP

When Michael Jackson wore a red leather jacket in the 'Thriller' video clip in 1983, it was a fashion statement that has since become iconic. Suddenly it was cool to wear coloured leather and this became a permanent fixture in fashion. His red leather jacket was made by Deborah Landis (who was married to the clip's director, John Landis) specifically for Jackson, who had a 26-inch waist. It had a distinctive V shape to its silhouette – the jacket was all about padding in the V-neck panelling and shoulders, and the collarless style became a teen must-have. The video clip follows a young couple whose night at the movies turns into a bloody thirsty zombie romp – with Jackson morphing from panther to zombie by the end of the clip. The video clip was one of the most expensive ever made, costing US$500,000. The jacket reportedly sold for US$1.8 million at auction in 2011.

1983

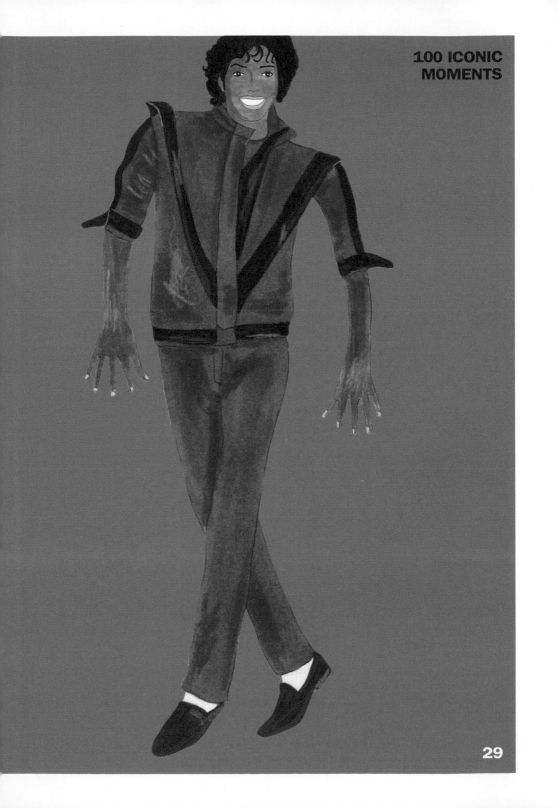

OLIVIA NEWTON-JOHN IN THE 'LET'S GET PHYSICAL' VIDEO CLIP

The '80s was the era of aerobics outfits and neon colours, where leg warmers, headbands and fitness found their way onto dance floors and fashion pages. It might have been Jane Fonda who made aerobics attire sexy in her exercise videos, but it was Olivia Newton-John who brought the style to the '80s video clip. The 1981 'Let's Get Physical' clip captured ath-leisure at its primal best, and ever since has inspired athletic trends, with urban fashionistas in 2016 still keen on fitted body suits and leotard-style tops. The video clip sees Newton-John cycling on a bike and wearing leggings and a headband in fluorescent colours, surrounded by fit and barely dressed men at the gym – it was tacky glam at its best.

1981

GRACE JONES KICKS ASS

Grace Jones is a style icon and provocateur who came to the world's attention as a model working in New York and Paris in the '70s for the likes of Yves Saint Laurent and Kenzo. Jones was one of the first models to subvert classic beauty with androgyny, and became a staple at Studio 54 in the '70s. While the '80s saw the rise of the supermodel and power dressing, Jones preferred to express her fashion voice via androgynous outfits – she was one part dominatrix and two shakes intimidating, wearing her hair cropped and her outfits tight. Jones signed to Island Records in the mid '70s and chased a music career, becoming a major act in the disco scene of the '80s. Jones' stage looks often included oversized shoulder pads, masculine silhouettes, a buzz cut with punk spike and tarantula-inspired fur coats. She's become the go-to woman for designers, photographers and artists looking for a fearless muse – everyone from Jean-Paul Goude to Azzedine Alaïa has channelled Jones' ballsy energy. She made Halston hooded scarves cool and always wore Philip Treacy headwear.

1970s

MADONNA IN THE 'LIKE A VIRGIN' VIDEO CLIP

Madonna's 1984 'Like a Virgin' video clip is an iconic pop culture moment for many reasons – it not only provocatively merged religious iconography like crucifixes and wedding gowns with punk rebellion (studded black belt and lace), it also presented Madonna as a virgin on a gondola in Italy, dancing sensually while being steered around Venetian canals. It was sexual, textual and it was political. The wedding dress Madonna wore in the clip only added to the controversy – a bride-to-be with sex on her mind was enough to cause headline hysteria. And it all helped push Madonna towards pop music domination. Madonna worked closely with stylist Maripol during this period, and the veil worn in the clip belonged to Maripol's friend Katsuko. The black rubber jewellery, chains and crucifixes were Maripol's idea – she was the art director for Italian fashion brand Fiorucci at the time. When Madonna wore the wedding dress from the clip at the VMA Awards in the same year and pointed to the camera while grabbing her crotch, it became an image that is still described today as controversial and empowering for women.

1984

SUZI QUATRO'S LEATHER LOOK

The '70s belonged to leather and when it came to women in rock 'n' roll, nobody wore a leather jumpsuit louder than American glam-rock singer Suzi Quatro. She brought a touch of *Happy Days* cool character 'The Fonz' to her feminine tough gal image (she even appeared on the show a few times as Leather Tuscadero) and says she was inspired to wear leather and sing rock 'n' roll by Elvis Presley, whom she discovered at the age of six. Quatro's leather outfits became a staple of her stage shows and image – the petite star being equal measures badass rocker and pioneer.

1970s

GWEN STEFANI'S HARAJUKU STYLE

Gwen Stefani shot to fame as the lead singer of Californian outfit No Doubt in the 1990s, and it didn't take long for the ska-reggae frontwoman to become a style fashion leader. But it was perhaps her 1995 foray into the world of Japan's Harajuku fashion that put Stefani under a new spotlight. Tokyo district Harajuku is famous for its extreme fashion styles, mixing second-hand with cyber fashion, Gothic Lolita or teen-bright ensembles. It became an obsession for the star who visited the area while on tour with her band. Stefani borrowed this style to inform her video clips and the way she dressed, and even launched a fashion label and a song inspired by the style, and used back-up dancers called the Harajuku girls. Her Gothic Lolita–influenced look intersected punk with rock and techno footnotes. Whichever way you look at it, Stefani was paying tribute (or in her words, a compliment) to the scene and copped flack for it, as she was criticised for cultural appropriation.

1990s

COURTNEY LOVE'S KINDER– WHORE LOOK

She might have once been married to Nirvana frontman Kurt Cobain, but Courtney Love put her own stamp on the '90s grunge scene as frontwoman of the band, Hole. She grew up on punk, and is credited for being the woman behind the 'kinderwhore' style, where girls wore ripped lace baby-doll dresses while playing guitar. The point was to encapsulate the irony of looking girly, but rocking like a badass. The kinderwhore look became iconic in the '90s, and was synonymous with grunge – it included ripped tights, slip lingerie worn as dresses and smeared kohl eyeliner and red lipstick, as well as vintage lace baby-doll dresses and tiaras. It was in your face and put thrift shopping high on the fashion agenda. While Love is more likely to be dressed in international couture houses these days, she still dresses with an element of punk rebellion.

1990s

ELVIS PRESLEY'S JUMPSUITS

Elvis Presley, the undisputed king of rock 'n' roll, loved a jumpsuit, although he never enjoyed wearing the same one twice. Jumpsuits were one-piece garments that had been worn by skydivers and racing-car drivers since the 1920s. Elvis first started to wear jumpsuits in 1970 – he repurposed this practical look for the stage with high Napoleonic collars, pointed sleeve cuffs, flared legs and glitter. The jumpsuit became the cornerstone of his stage persona at his Vegas shows. He loved rhinestone and metal-studded jumpsuit varieties and wore them until his death in 1977. Bill Belew designed The Black Conquistador jumpsuit for Elvis, complete with a vampire-like cape and elaborate embroidery stitched by Gene Doucette. One of Elvis's most famous jumpsuits was 1973's American Eagle, worn during his Vegas reign, which featured the iconic bird emblazoned brightly on the back.

1970s

DAVID BOWIE'S MCQUEEN COAT

Hailed an iconic look from the '90s, the Union Jack coat designed by Alexander McQueen for the music icon David Bowie in 1996 was a collaborative effort between the pair. It was a below-the-knee frock coat made entirely of a Union Jack, using deliberately distressed fabric. Bowie was so impressed with the coat he wore it on the cover of his *Earthling* album, on the accompanying tour and to the VH1 Awards in the same year – its image is now etched in a corner of '90s pop moments. McQueen was still relatively unknown at the time, and the original collaboration turned out to be the first of many.

1996

ADAM ANT'S PIRATE PUNK STYLE

Adam Ant, leader singer of Adam and the Ants, was an '80s fashion hero, loved for his post-punk new wave stance, pirate cool and sequined attempts at bringing a bit of Robin Hood to music. He was proudly punk, a touch dandy and referenced military fashion before it became cool to do so. He rocked period glam with a touch of Napoleonic charm. His look in the video clip for Adam and the Ants' hit single 'Stand and Deliver' was pirate cool meets '80s new wave soundtrack, and it catapulted Ant's dandy highwayman look to fashion fame. Ant often shopped at Vivienne Westwood and Malcolm McLaren's Sex Shop in London in the mid '70s, wearing clothes that shocked, always seeing beauty in the forbidden clothing they sold. McLaren was also managing Ant's band at the time. Ant wore vintage Westwood kilts, tight leather pants, and often performed topless with a smeared white paint line across his face. He spent the '70s hanging out with Goth vixens like Siouxsie Sioux from The Banshees. He was a pop star ahead of his time, adored for the way he merged feminine and masculine fashion, and steered it to the top of the charts.

1980s

100 ICONIC
MOMENTS

FASHION A-LISTERS

AUDREY HEPBURN IN *BREAKFAST AT TIFFANY'S*

When Audrey Hepburn, playing call-girl Holly Golightly, stood outside Tiffany's Fifth Avenue wearing a black dress in the opening scene of the 1961 movie *Breakfast at Tiffany's*, it instantly became one of fashion's greatest moments. Hepburn was wearing a black floor-length Italian satin sheath designed by Givenchy, along with long black gloves and complete with pearl choker and cigarette holder. It captured Parisian femininity on the streets on New York City. Even though Hepburn's relationship with Givenchy began eight years prior to *Breakfast at Tiffany's* when her agent sent her to Givenchy's Paris studio to create a wardrobe for her role in *Sabrina*, it was this moment that put the petite starlet in the spotlight as an icon for effortless chic and style.

1961

FACTORY GIRL EDIE SEDGWICK

American socialite, actress and fashion model Edie Sedgwick was dubbed an 'It girl' by *Vogue* USA in the '60s. Moving to New York in 1964, by 1965 Sedgwick was a regular in Andy Warhol's Factory scene and appeared in 12 of Warhol's short films. Sedgwick's cool '60s style and femme fatale appeal defined the fashion of that New York era – it was all about black opaque tights, striped t-shirts and boatneck tees, mini-dresses, chandelier earrings and heavy black eyeliner. She regularly appeared in fashion magazines with her crop of dyed blonde hair and kohl-rimmed eyes, spawning a new look for young women to replicate. Yet she was a troubled starlet who battled drug and alcohol addiction. The film *Factory Girl*, starring Sienna Miller, was based on Sedgwick's life story as a free spirit who struggled with addiction. Bob Dylan reportedly wrote 'Just Like A Woman' about her.

1960s

KATE MIDDLETON IN MCQUEEN

Kate Middleton's 2011 wedding gown will go down as the most talked about in recent history. She chose Alexander McQueen's creative director Sarah Burton to design the dress and has remained a loyal client of the iconic British brand ever since. It was the fashion world's best-kept secret, and not even Middleton's parents knew what their daughter would wear on her wedding day. The dreamy gown wooed with its full skirt made of hand-cut English and French Chantilly lace, a veil constructed of layers of ivory silk tulle with hand-embroidered flowers and a fitted bodice with the padding at the hips that is iconic of the late Alexander McQueen's own personal design style. The dress was seen as an homage to Grace Kelly's wedding dress – a flattering design that was modest, contemporary and dramatic, all at once. The dress has also been compared to the one worn by Queen Elizabeth II when she married Prince Philip in 1947.

2011

CLAIRE DANES IN ZAC POSEN AT THE 2016 MET GALA

American designer Zac Posen made a gown straight out of a modern fairytale for Claire Danes' appearance at the Met Gala in 2016. The strapless gown was made to celebrate the year's Costume Institute exhibition, 'Manus x Machina: Fashion in an Age of Technology'. Posen wove fibre-optic cables into the fabric of the dress and lit it up with a flick of the switch hidden inside. The fashion designer fused the best of both worlds with this dress, giving a generous nod to modern technology with the L.E.D. lighting that made the gown glow in the dark, while the shape of the gown was a classic Cinderella silhouette.

2016

CARRIE BRADSHAW IN VERSACE'S MILLE FEUILLE DRESS

When Carrie Bradshaw, played by Sarah Jessica Parker, wore a grey Mille Feuille dress by Versace in *Sex and the City* season 6, it became a hyped talking point in fashion circles. Bradshaw was an American girl in Paris; it was the city of her dreams, but she was stood up by her boyfriend on her first night in town while wearing the Mille Feuille dress. At least she looked amazing. The memorable gown (which cost US$80,000) looked at its most glamorous when Bradshaw sat on her bed with the many layers of fabric spilling all around her – the security of warmth she wasn't feeling from her flame! The dress was named after the famous layered cake and, according to the series stylist Patricia Field, was chosen to mimic the rise and fall and many complicated layers of Bradshaw's romantic relationships.

2004

58

MARILYN MONROE'S IVORY WHITE COCKTAIL DRESS

In 1954, Marilyn Monroe was in New York filming a scene for Billy Wilder's *The Seven Year Itch*. A scene from that movie has become one of the most iconic of American cinema – that of Monroe's white ivory cocktail dress blowing up over her hips while she stood over a subway grate. The photo was taken by Sam Shaw, and apparently it was his idea for the flying skirt to be captured in a film still. The halter-like bodice with its plunging neckline was made of pleated fabrics. At the time Monroe was married to athlete Joe DiMaggio who apparently wasn't a fan of the dress, but it became a cornerstone of fashion sexiness and cocktail must-have – the silhouette ever-present in modern couture today.

1954

KATE HUDSON'S BOHO CHIC IN *ALMOST FAMOUS*

Kate Hudson's wardrobe in Cameron Crowe's 2000 movie *Almost Famous* was curated by costume designer Betsy Heimann. The movie's '70s bohemian look, all flared jeans and band t-shirts, was channelled via Heimann's finds at thrift stores across the country. Heimann used photographs of Neil Young's 1973 tour taken by good friend and rock photographer Joel Bernstein to inform her hunter-gatherer fashion decisions, which were one part rock 'n' roll and two shakes '70s throwback. The famous Penny Lane coat worn by Hudson was made from a second-hand upholstery fabric and the shaggy collar was assembled from a rug. Hudson's look in the film helped to create a boho revival in 2000s fashion.

2000

CARRIE BRADSHAW IN OSCAR DE LA RENTA

When it comes to memorable fashion moments, hit TV show *Sex and The City* played a huge role in building the sartorial foundations of the '90s – it had women worldwide glued to the screen waiting to see what the four leading ladies would wear next. In season 6 of the series, Carrie Bradshaw, played by Sarah Jessica Parker, drools over a hot-pink Oscar de la Renta cocktail dress, lusting after the sleeveless silk faille and full-skirted skirt with black patent leather bow belt. Her then boyfriend gifts her the dress, and Carrie ends up at a McDonald's wearing that fabulous Oscar de la Renta gown, eating fries alongside her boyfriend. It's not the first time Bradshaw wore de la Renta– another darling moment was when she took part in the *Vogue* magazine wedding dress shoot on the show wearing a de la Renta gown.

2003

MARLON BRANDO'S BAD BOY COOL

When Marlon Brando appeared in the 1953 film *The Wild One* wearing a black leather biker jacket, it became an iconic image that would influence youth culture for decades to come. Brando in his leather jacket was outlaw and sexy all at once. Brando played Johnny Strabler, a member of a motorcycle gang called The Black Rebel Motorcycle Club, who made the biker tough bad-boy look cool. The jacket he wore was known as the Perfecto. Created by Irving Schott from New York's outerwear company Schott Bros, the jacket became the epitome of cool once Brando wore it. As one of the silver screen's sexiest leading men, Brando walked the fine line between handsome and rebel.

1953

NATALIE PORTMAN IN GIVENCHY

When Natalie Portman arrived at the amfAR Cinema Against AIDS dinner at Cannes in 2008 wearing a sculptural white Givenchy gown it became one of the evening's most memorable red carpet looks. The origami-like folds and birds-of-a-feather allure were potentially the ultimate precursor that she would take out an Academy Award for psychological thriller *Black Swan* a few years later. This ruffled white gown put both Portman and Givenchy's Creative Director, Riccardo Tisci, in the fashion spotlight. Portman also wore Givenchy on another memorable occasion, donning the original Audrey Hepburn black dress from *Breakfast at Tiffany's* in a *Harper's Bazaar* USA cover shoot in 2006.

2008

LUISA, MARCHESA CASATI

Luisa, Marchesa Casati was an heiress, arts patroness and Italian socialite who led an unusual life – she loved séances, adored the occult, wore peacock feathers, chains and was often naked underneath a fur coat. And all before World War I. She was the scandalous woman of the Belle Époque, who inspired fashion greats like Alexander McQueen and Karl Lagerfeld almost a century later. When living in Venice, she met Paul Poiret, an art deco stylist and artist who dressed her like a chandelier. She housed a private zoo in her palazzo on the Grand Canal filled with albino crows and snakes. She became a muse for Pablo Picasso and Jean Cocteau, was photographed by Man Ray and even inspired the Marchesa fashion label founded by Georgia Chapman and Keren Craig in 2004. Casati was a lasting muse, captured at her most eccentric in Joseph Paget-Frederick's painting of her walking two leopards.

1900s

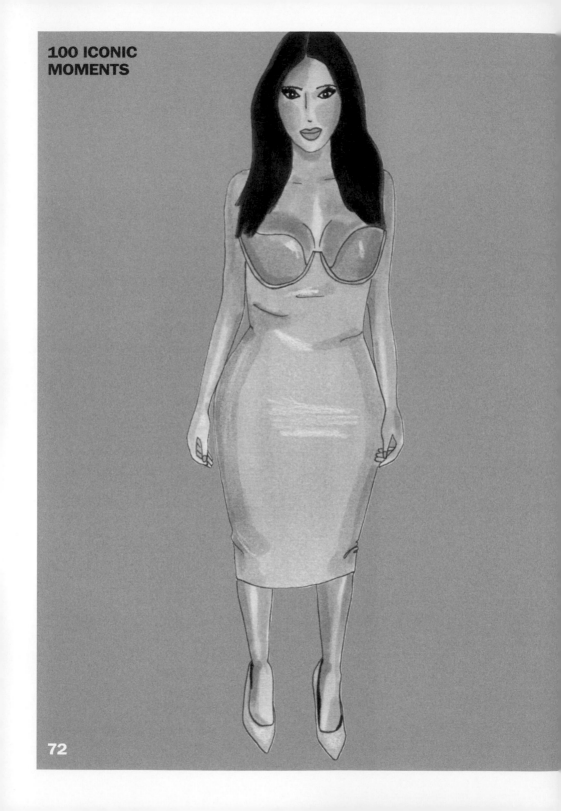

KIM KARDASHIAN IN ATSUKO KUDO'S LATEX DRESS

The black dominatrix-inspired corset dress Kim Kardashian West wore in 2014 was created by designer Atsuko Kudo. Kardashian loved the dress so much she wore the same style, but in pink, to a perfume launch later in the same year. The dress clung to Kardashian's endless curves in an iconic fashion moment. The reality TV star and mogul put latex in the couture spotlight, taking the material from the fetish space into the mainstream, with high street brands following in the lucrative Kardashian footsteps. Many other stars followed Kardashian's lead including model Bella Hadid and *Transformers* actress Nicola Peltz who were both spotted on red carpets wearing the original black Atsuko Kudo design.

2014

100 ICONIC MOMENTS

HIGH
FASHION

CHANEL'S LITTLE BLACK DRESS

The fact that we now consider the little black dress to be a wardrobe essential is owed in part to French fashion designer Coco Chanel, who in 1926 included a little black dress in her collection. Until then, the black dress had been associated with mourning, but Chanel took it from funeral outfit and created a classic fashion look. Perhaps the key moment in the little black dress's transformation was when Chanel's illustration of her design was published in *Vogue* USA. The illustrated dress had a straight silhouette that ran to calf-length, and *Vogue* dubbed it Chanel's Model T, referencing the democratic Ford model car of the era, as they predicted the dress would become a fashion staple. The little black dress was seen as accessible regardless of social status and would become a uniform for the fashion-conscious woman – it still hasn't lost its sartorial power and continues to be the dress of choice for women worldwide.

1926

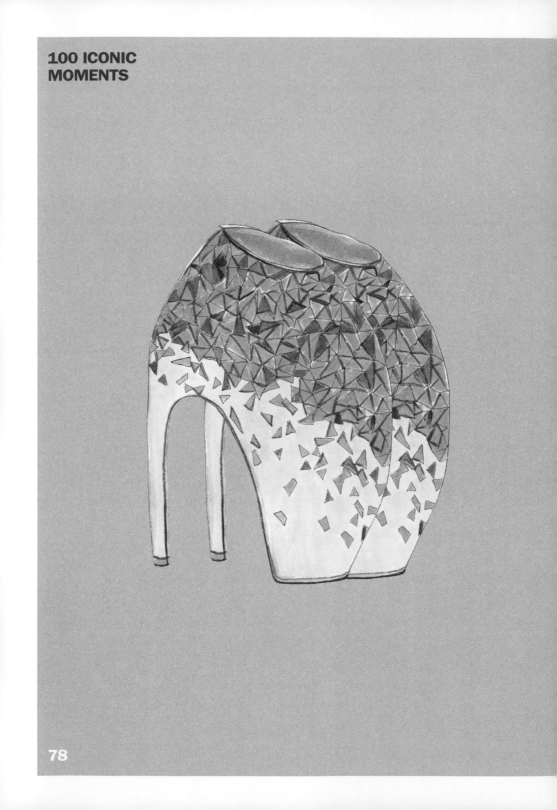

ALEXANDER MCQUEEN'S ARMADILLO SHOES

The fantastical armadillo shoe created by the late Alexander McQueen was one of the British fashion designer's hallmark moments. There were just 21 pairs created solely for the designer's 2010 Spring/Summer collection, and it was a turning point for the reluctant star. McQueen's vision was one of fantasy overriding reality – the shoes were 30 centimetres (12 inches) in height, and merged animal-like prints with ballerina poses that looked impractical yet poised. They were strikingly beautiful on the runway, making models look like sensual sci-fi creatures. Each pair of shoes was handmade in Italy, a process that took five days and involved 30 people. The reptilian shoes created a fashion buzz. Britain's Daphne Guinness was the first off the runway to walk in a pair of armadillo shoes, but it was Lady Gaga who purchased three of the collection.

2010

YSL'S LE SMOKING SUIT

When Yves Saint Laurent introduced a tuxedo-style suit for women in 1966 it became the epitome of Parisian sexy chic, a touch androgynous, a bit dominatrix and a whole lot of woman all at once. Catherine Deneuve was the suit's first customer, wearing it in 1967. It had been banned from various restaurants in Paris, where women were expected to dine in skirts, not pants. But it was fashion photographer Helmut Newton who made the suit famous, photographing it for French *Vogue* in 1975. The suit has been replicated over the decades by many other fashion designers, often borrowing from YSL's original template combining minimalism and androgyny. Word has it Saint Laurent was influenced by the avant-garde style of artist Niki de Saint Phalle, who was an artist in the '50s and who reportedly wore men's suits paired with heels – like film stars Greta Garbo and Marlene Dietrich in the '30s before her.

1966

DIANE VON FÜRSTENBERG'S WRAP DRESS

When fashion designer Diane von Fürstenberg arrived in New York in the 1970s with a suitcase full of jersey fabric, she used it to make her now cult-favourite wrap dress in 1974. The simple design became a hit among the Studio 54 crowd and resonated with women of all shapes and sizes for its effortlessly chic figure-hugging style that complemented a woman's curves. Cybill Shepherd wore a red wrap dress in Martin Scorsese's *Taxi Driver*. The dress featured a low-neck, geometric pattern and tie-waist – it was a sultry number and a classy act. Michelle Obama chose a DVF wrap dress with a floral print for her first White House Christmas.

1974

THE BURBERRY TRENCH COAT

The history of the trench coat goes back to the 1850s with both Burberry and Aquascutum, a heritage British brand, claiming its creation. Thomas Burberry invented gabardine fabric, which he used to make trench coats, in 1879. He designed an army officer's raincoat using the fabric for the UK's War Office in 1901, which ultimately became the Burberry trench. It was film star Humphrey Bogart who truly made the trench a fashion icon when he wore one in 1942's *Casablanca*. Bogart's look in the movie immortalised the smart-yet-casual silhouette of the coat, rather than the military status it had enjoyed to that point. The Burberry trench is instantly recognisable by its check-print lining – a combination of camel, red, ivory and black. The trench still finds a comfy place in runway shows and is relevant to the modern man (and woman). A Burberry trench coat takes three weeks to construct and is made in Castleford, a town in the north of England.

1901

HERMÈS BAGS

The luxury French brand Hermès was founded in 1837 by German-born and French-raised Thierry Hermès, who initially made luxury harnesses, bridles and saddles for noblemen's horses, later introducing a bag designed to carry the saddles. The company made their first leather handbag for women in 1922, and redesigned it as the *sac à dèpêches* bag in the 1930s. This narrow briefcase became famous when Grace Kelly carried one in Hitchcock's classic film, *To Catch a Thief.* Kelly became a fan, and the bag was renamed after her. In the '80s, the company introduced the Birkin bag, named after actress Jane Birkin, by far its most popular design. It was created out of a need for a larger bag than the Kelly version. Apparently the CEO of Hermès sat next to Birkin on a flight and noticed the contents of Birkin's bag fall out – prompting the actress to explain it was hard to find a weekend bag. The iconic bags are made from saltwater crocodile skin and sell for up to US$250,000. It's the ultimate social status accessory. Each bag is hand-sewn and can take up to two days to make.

1922

MANOLO BLAHNIK'S STILETTO HEELS

Manolo Blahnik was born in the Canary Islands, but moved to Paris to become a set designer in 1968 – although an introduction to famous *Vogue* USA editor Diana Vreeland turned him towards shoe design. He collaborated on his first pair of heels with Swinging Sixties designer Ossie Clark in 1972, and opened a boutique selling his shoe designs in 1973. His designs helped revive interest in the stiletto heel and he achieved wide-spread fame in the '90s as the favourite shoe designer of Carrie Bradshaw, the shoe-obsessed main character in cult TV show *Sex and the City*. Even though Blahnik isn't formally trained in shoe-making, he designs every pair himself. Some of his most striking styles include the BB Pump, Swan Pump, Campari Pump and Chaos Sandal, and he recently collaborated with Rihanna on a range.

1977

CHRISTIAN DIOR'S 'THE NEW LOOK'

French fashion couturier Christian Dior debuted his fashion house in 1947 with a collection titled 'The New Look'. His collection focused on rounded shoulders, cinched waist and a full skirt. It was all about creating a figure-eight silhouette – tall shoulders, tiny waistline and rounded hips for feminine elegance – and heralded a change in the way women dressed after World War II, with femininity replacing the war period's masculine silhouettes. Then editor-in-chief of *Harper's Bazaar* Carmel Snow declared Dior's unique dresses as the 'new look' the fashion world had been waiting for. Gone were the days of rations and uniforms – Dior was hailed a hero for bringing back a feminised elegance to women's wear. This look continues to be referenced in fashion, with everyone from Viktor & Rolf to Prada repurposing this look with modern twists in recent collections.

1947

MULBERRY'S ALEXA BAG

The Mulberry Alexa handbag is named after Brit
It girl Alexa Chung, who is a model, TV presenter,
author and contributing editor at British *Vogue*.
Chung used to get around carrying the Elkington,
a Mulberry's men's briefcase. This inspired
Mulberry to create the Alexa, which combines the
British It girl's mix of boyish charm and cool-girl
style. Naming bags after famous women isn't
anything new – in the '50s Hermès renamed their
classic *sac à dépêches* the Kelly bag after actress
Grace Kelly and created and named the Birkin
for Jane Birkin, the '60s actress and model. Now
there's a handbag muse for the new millennium;
Mulberry brought Chung's eccentric edge,
elegance and modern-day romance to the Alexa,
which became one of their most popular styles.

2010

PRADA'S SPRING/ SUMMER COATS

For her 2014 Spring/Summer collection, Miuccia Prada created coats emblazoned with a feminist statement designed to inspire women. These coats were the epitome of fashion meets art, with cartoon-inspired visages, bold colour and fur adorned with crystals, and her runway models were like fierce girl gangs. Prada is a leader in the extraordinary – she's an intellectual who happens to be a fashion designer (she was famously a member of Italy's communist party), and her collections are modern, risky and daring. In this collection, art set the agenda. The designer commissioned a series of artists including El Mac, Mesa, Gabriel Specter, Stinkfish, Jeanne Detallante and Pierre Mornet to create large murals for the runway show as well. It was all about women and strength, a passionately feminist theme to her trailblazing collection.

2014

VIVIENNE WESTWOOD & MALCOLM MCLAREN'S PIRATE LOOK

Vivienne Westwood and Malcolm McLaren are British fashion designers who brought punk and new wave fashion to the mainstream. They showed their first runway collection, titled 'The Pirate Collection' in London and then Paris in 1981. The collection captured the essence of the new wave romantic era, and they showed baggy pirate trousers, striped tops and trainers. The dynamic British duo moved beyond the days of punk in this collection with a mix of Native American influences and ethnic prints. It was all about mixing an 18th-century style with flowing layers and the famous Squiggle print that became perennially 'Westwood'.

1981

ISABELLA BLOW, FASHION INSIDER

She was one of Britain's most famous faces, as known for her eccentric headwear as she was for her adoration of couture and fashion. She had a love affair with hats, and once said that dressing without a hat was like not being dressed at all. Milliner Philip Treacy, who made many of her hats, also became her confidante. She discovered Alexander McQueen when he was a fashion student at Central Saint Martins College of Art and Design and was Anna Wintour's assistant when she moved to New York in the '80s, even becoming a Warhol Factory Girl for a while. By 1986 she had returned to London and was working for Michael Roberts – the then fashion editor of *Tatler* and *Sunday Times* 'Style' magazine. She became the fashion director of *Tatler* in the 2000s. Blow's fashion style and ability to spot talent became her forte – she was post-modern, at times medieval and Gothic-like, and always had an ability to be groundbreaking. She was a patron of the arts as well. She told British *Vogue* that 'fashion is a vampiric thing, it's the hoover on your brain. That's why I wear the hats, to keep everyone away from me. They say, "Oh, can I kiss you?" I say, "No, thank you very much. That's why I've worn the hat. Goodbye."' She sadly took her own life at 48.

2000s

HALSTON

Roy Halston Frowick, known as Halston, was
never short of high-profile followers. He created
the pillbox hat Jackie Kennedy was wearing when
JFK was assassinated in 1963, and moved into
designing clothes shortly after. His fashion label
was big in the '70s with fans including Elizabeth
Taylor, Bianca Jagger and Liza Minnelli. Best-
known for his minimalist clothing designs made
of cashmere and ultra-suede, his dresses could
be found on the fashion set dancing at Studio 54.
Vogue credits him with popularising kaftans and
jersey halter-neck dresses, but he became most
famous for his ultra-suede shirtdress, a bestseller
among celebrities of the era. Halston sold his
company in 1973, but he remained principal designer
into the '80s. While the Halston Heritage brand
continues today, it's now Halston in name only.

1970s

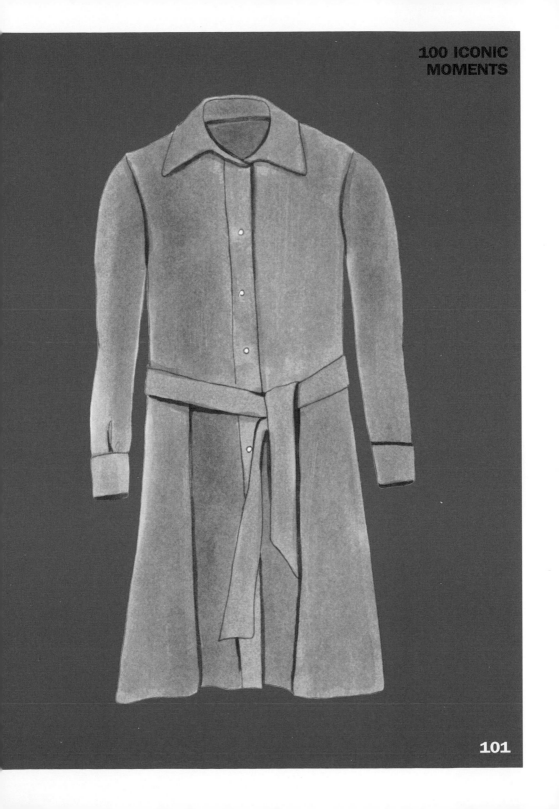

ANNA SUI'S GRUNGE COLLECTION

In 1993, Anna Sui riffed off the Seattle grunge bandwagon with a collection that celebrated the slacker scene and feasted on its nihilistic viewpoint. She was a fashion designer from Detroit, who had made her runway debut in 1991. In this collection, she sent the top models of the time down the runway, including Kate Moss, Helena Christensen and Naomi Campbell, wearing Doc Marten–inspired lace-up boots and vibrant stripes that weren't dissimilar to what Kurt Cobain often wore. A year earlier Marc Jacobs had also sent models down the runway wearing beanies, flannel shirts and printed granny dresses, shifting grunge from radio play to runway in a few badass moves.

1993

COMME DES GARÇONS' OVERSIZED LOOK

Japanese trailblazer Rei Kawakubo made her fashion debut in 1981 with her label Comme des Garçons. She quickly became the leader in a new sartorial journey, which included avant-garde designs, oversized shirts, dresses and pants, and outfits that were predominantly black. She was part of a wave of designers who preferred oversized garments, challenging the conventional notions of beauty and shape.

1981

ISSEY MIYAKE'S BUSTIER

Japanese designer Issey Miyake likes to experiment with unusual materials in fashion, from plastic to rope and paper. He's often conceptual in his approach. His 1980 red bustier was made from metal, opaque synthetic polymer resin and polyester, and made its debut during Miyake's 1980 Autumn/Winter Paris collection. It has been hailed an iconic fashion moment because it provoked the notion of fashion as body-conscious art. The wearable bustier was an experimental garment that Grace Jones wore while on tour in 1980. It was shiny red in texture and looked more like sculpture than clothing.

1980

ELSA SCHIAPARELLI, QUEEN OF FASHION

Renowned Queen of Fashion Elsa Schiaparelli was born into an aristocratic Roman family, but was based in Paris where she became a rival of Coco Chanel and friends with prominent surrealists like Jean Cocteau and Salvador Dalí – even collaborating with Dalí on her 1937 lobster dress. Schiaparelli became known for her style between the two World Wars and was inspired to design by mentor and friend, couturier Paul Poiret. She was not trained in pattern making, relying on instinct and impulse when it came to dress design. Having decided to try her luck in the fashion business in 1926, Schiaparelli launched her first collection in 1927. One of the first fashion designers to use rayon, thick velvets, see-through raincoats, wrap dresses and trompe l'oeil bows, Schiaparelli loved to work with embroidery. Her surrealist influences appeared in her work through the use of whimsical buttons, feathers and sequins for an exaggerated beauty. Her business closed down in 1954.

1920s

SONIA RYKIEL

Sonia Rykiel became the first fashion designer to put the 'poor boy sweater' in the fashion spotlight. The French fashion icon, who launched her brand in 1968, became known for her loose-fitting clothes, sweaters and for employing some of the biggest names in the business to strut the catwalk for her – Helena Christensen, Tyra Banks and Georgia May Jagger to name a few. She adored stripes and frequently used pops of colour in her runway collections. Actress Brigitte Bardot wore Rykiel's sweaters, as did singer and actress Françoise Hardy in the '60s, famously wearing a Rykiel striped top on the cover of *Elle Paris*. Rykiel made clothes that were cool, chic and felt like a Parisian student rebellion.

1968

KATE MOSS ON THE GUCCI RUNWAY IN 1996

After Tom Ford took over as creative director at Gucci in the mid '90s, he enlisted Kate Moss to walk the runway in his much talked about 1996 collection. It became an iconic moment in the Italian brand's history, which had experienced tumultuous times in the '80s with internal politics following the death of Maurizio Gucci, and the resulting bad press. Ford's collection was all about sexy and slinky cut-out dresses in seductive black, and keyhole gowns in white, with Moss appearing on the catwalk in a barely-there top with exposed midriff and elegant pants. Ford revamped the design house over a 10-year reign from 1994 to 2004 – he revolutionised the designs and worked with fashion photographer Mario Testino, who immortalised the minimalist glory with some mind-blowing campaign shots of power suits, plunging necklines and girl power.

1996

PACO RABANNE'S METAL MINI-DRESS

Paco Rabanne began as a jewellery designer before turning to fashion. His first fashion collection in 1966 featured his famous mini-dress – made out of plastic and metal, it was daring and groundbreaking. The look was futuristic, '60s go-go and intergalactic all at once. Barbarella, played by Jane Fonda in the eponymous film, wore a metal-mesh outfit by Rabanne, while French singer and actress Françoise Hardy was also a fan. Prior to creating this collection Rabanne worked for Nina Ricci, Pierre Cardin, Givenchy and Balenciaga designing jewellery.

1966

100 ICONIC
MOMENTS

HIGH
STREET

MINISKIRT

The miniskirt raised eyebrows and hemlines in the '60s, with London fashion designer Mary Quant and Parisian designer Andrè Courrèges first bringing the skirt to the world's attention. Who actually invented the miniskirt has caused debate over the decades – British designer John Bates was named the first by a British Vogue journalist, while YSL and Pierre Cardin were raising hemlines around the same time as Quant. History has it that Quant took the idea from the 1964 designs by Courrèges and, liking the shorter styles, made them even shorter for her boutique, Bazaar. She also named the skirt after her favourite car, the Mini. The miniskirt became a cornerstone of the Swinging Sixties and everyone from Brigitte Bardot to Marianne Faithfull wore one.

1960s

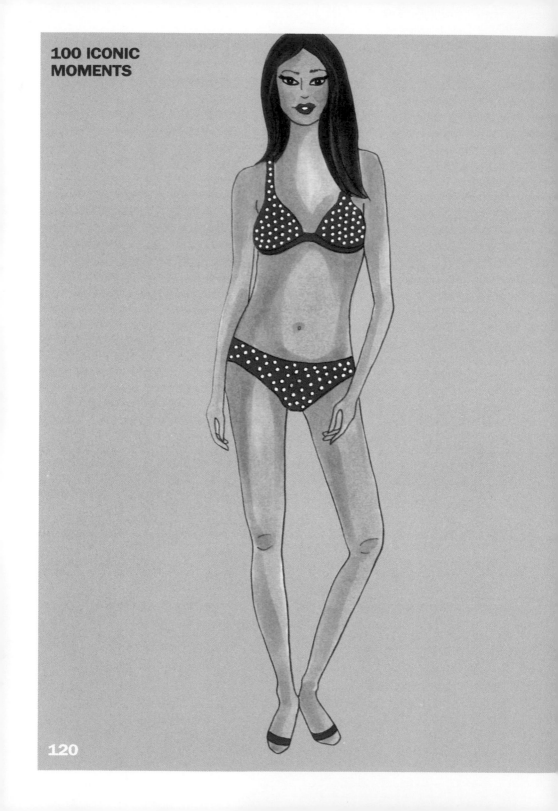

BIKINI

In 1946, Parisian engineer turned lingerie designer Louis Réard came up with the term 'bikini' to describe his company's two-piece swimsuit. It was named after Bikini Atoll, where a nuclear bomb had been tested – Réard thought his design would be similarly shocking. Ever since, the bikini has been an essential of summer-time fun. The two-piece swimsuit had been around since the 1930s, but prior to Réard it didn't reveal the navel and was more modest in shape, with high-waisted bottoms and halter-style tops. It wasn't until the '60s that the bikini really took off – with Raquel Welch and Ursula Andress famously wearing bikinis on screen. The Vatican declared the bikini's skin-baring creation a sin, but the two-piece has become a fashion hit and mainstay of beach life. From itsy-bitsy polka-dot varieties to frilly two-piece creations by Missoni in 1969, the humble bikini is a curve-hugging and revealing outfit that took the concept of the bathing costume from conservative to wow in a few snips of fabric.

1946

MAXI DRESS

The maxi dress made a floor-sweeping statement at the tail end of the '60s, when the fashion world had had enough of the miniskirt and wanted a new direction. In 1968, *The New York Times* featured a cotton maxi dress by Oscar de la Renta for the Elizabeth Arden Salon (he began his tenure designing for Elizabeth Arden in 1963) and it would only be a matter of time before the likes of YSL, Biba, Halston and Dior would also add maxi dresses to their collections. By the late '60s, and just as hippie free love was about to shake the foundations of the early '70s, bohemian gals adopted the maxi for its free-spirited and flowing silhouette. The style was often rendered in fabrics with bold Indian- and African-inspired prints.

1960s

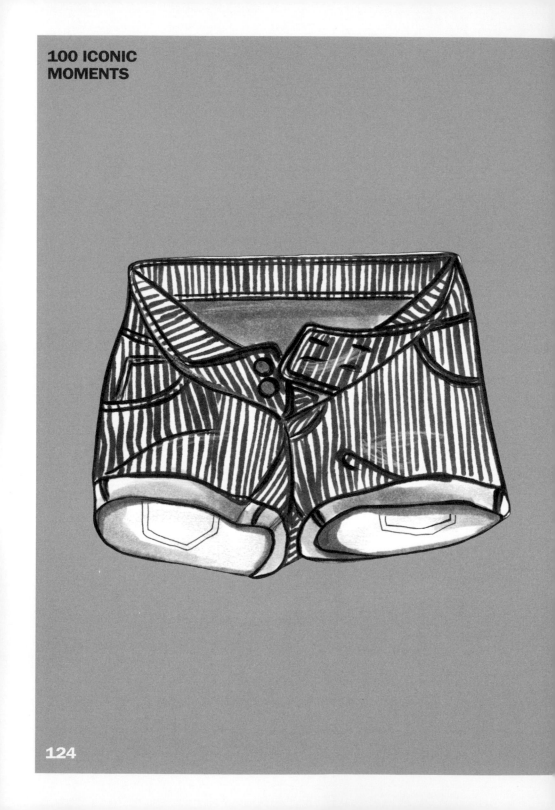

HOTPANTS

Hotpants, like miniskirts, were the cornerstone of the '60s. UK fashion designer Mary Quant, who made the style popular, says we can thank the girls on King's Road, London, for bringing the world's attention to the booty-hugging shorts, which were made possible by the invention of polyester. By 1971, hotpants were at the peak of their popularity – the stretchy fabric perfect for dancing to the disco beat. Even airlines embraced the look, with companies such as Southwest making hotpants and go-go boots part of their hostess uniforms.

1971

DENIM JEANS

In 1871, Jacob W. Davis and Levi Strauss invented Levi's blue jeans, although the name 'jean' actually comes from the city of Genoa in Italy, where the original jean fabric of cotton corduroy was manufactured. Now made from denim or dungaree, jeans have since become a staple of teen culture, adult life and runway fashion shows. But they had a humble beginning, starting as a work uniform worn by farmers and miners, before cowboys, rebels, rock stars and movie stars started embracing the style. The classic 501 style was Levi's first pair of jeans, although it's been through multiple reincarnations since then. John Wayne wore a pair of 501s in the 1939 film *Stagecoach*, but it was Marlon Brando who gave the same style of jeans sex appeal in 1953's *The Wild One*. And then there was Paul Newman in 1963's *Hud*, who wore double denim long before it became a thing in fashion. Ever since then, denim has found a place in popular culture and on the runway, from the denim-clad Ramones to Jean Paul Gaultier, Givenchy and Maison Margiela all purposefully creating runway shows that nodded to jeans.

1871

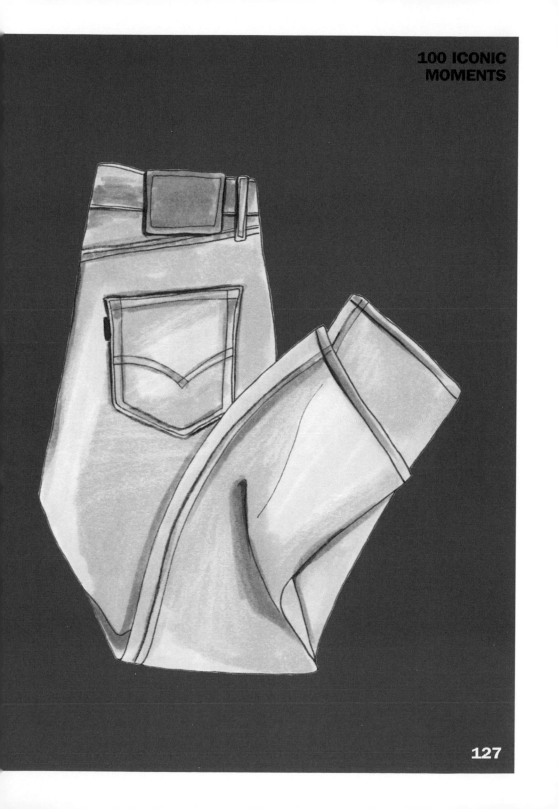

SEERSUCKER SUIT

Seersucker is a thin, light cotton fabric that has its origins in India, and was especially popular in warmer climates during the British Colonial era. The fabric is known for its irregular warp and is often made in pinstripe. It wasn't until seersucker made its way to the USA that the fabric truly became popular. Miles Davis wore a seersucker suit in the '50s while Gregory Peck made it famous as lawyer Atticus Finch in the classic 1962 movie *To Kill a Mockingbird*. The lightweight fabric also found its way into swimwear trunks and shirts by the 1950s. Nick Cave sang about the seersucker suit in *I Had a Dream Joe* in the '90s. It's cool, sharp, elegant and remains prevalent in fashion today.

1950s

KAFTAN

The kaftan originated in Mesopotamia, an ancient Middle Eastern empire that covered parts of modern Iraq, Turkey and Syria, as a coat or overdress worn by men and women, often made in silk or cotton. It became popular in western culture in the '60s when the style was adopted by the bohemian set, who always wore kaftans with the ethnic prints of its origins. It was one part peasant, two shakes hippie and was seen everywhere at the Woodstock festival in 1969. Kaftans were generally worn with long flowing hair, wide-brimmed hats and sunglasses. These days, fashion designers still love the kaftan and it appears regularly in resort wear collections, and often finds a spot by the beach.

1960s

BIAS CUT DRESS

French fashion designer Madeleine Vionnet popularised the bias cut dress in the 1920s. The style of dress uses fabric that has been cut obliquely or diagonally across the grain, giving gowns a slinkier silhouette. Vionnet became known as the queen of the bias cut, and the dress style revolutionised the 1930s. Her backless evening dress with bias cut lines was inspired by Ancient Grecian dresses, with the romantic silhouette highlighting the wearer's curves. Vionnet's dresses were worn by the likes of film stars Greta Garbo and Marlene Dietrich.

1920s

BELL-BOTTOMS

Bell-bottom pants were big in the '60s and '70s. The pants were figure hugging to the knee and then flared out in the shape of a bell. Made of corduroy, denim and velvet in the hippie '60s and polyester and satin in the disco '70s, nobody wore the pants more proudly than the cool kids in the late '60s and early '70s era – think Mick Jagger, Twiggy, Jimi Hendrix and the Woodstock crowd. British fashion designer Mary Quant brought a flared pant to her 1972 collection while Sonny and Cher made the look popular on US television.

1960s

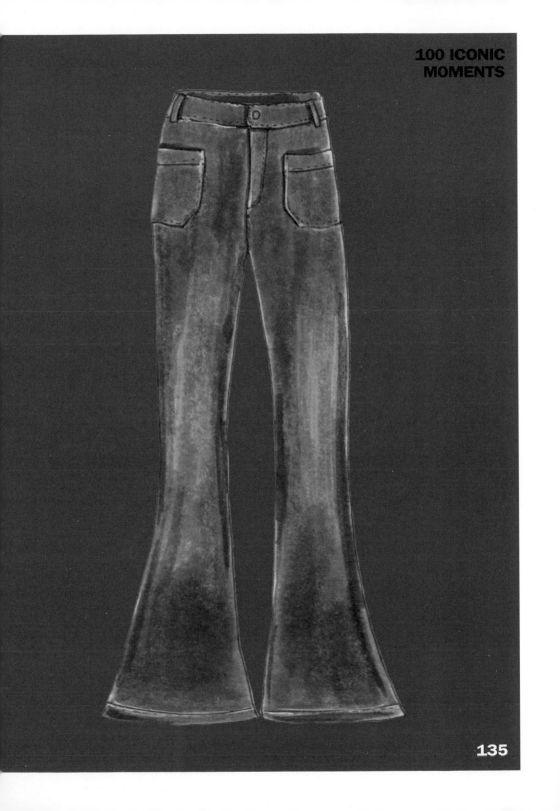

PUFFBALL SKIRT

The puffball skirt, otherwise known as the bubble skirt, had its heyday in the '80s. Featuring layer after layer of ruffles, the puffball took its silhouette from a '40s New Look–style dress but added '80s oomph. French fashion icon Christian Lacroix made the puffball a staple in his fantasy-like collections in the '80s and Princess Diana wore a black-and-white striped puffball skirt in 1987. The skirt still finds a puffy place in couture today.

1980

RAH-RAH SKIRT

The rah-rah skirt was big in the '80s – a fashion favourite among new-wavers who loved the short skirt with its rah-rah flounce. The design was originally worn by cheerleaders, but was adopted by teenagers worldwide in the '80s who claimed it as their era's new miniskirt. Madonna and Cyndi Lauper were early adopters of the rah-rah skirt and it was often worn with fishnet tights, sneakers and big hair.

1980s

POWER SUIT

The skirt-and-jacket power suit belonged to
the '80s and everyone from Giorgio Armani to
Nina Ricci put it on the catwalk with a sensual
masculine strut. It was Melanie Griffith in Working
Girl (she later earned an Oscar for the movie) who
made power dressing in a power suit glamorous.
But it was way back in 1932 when fashion designer
Marcel Rochas first created a wide-shouldered suit
for women, nodding to early working gals who knew
there was more to a woman's life than the home.

1980s

BOMBER JACKET

The bomber jacket dates back to World War I, when pilots needed jackets to protect against the cold weather, as cockpits at the time were open to the elements. These days the bomber jacket is more fashion than military attire. While its heart and soul remains the classic military silhouette, the jackets are now more often made of silk and satin than the sheepskin-padded varieties that dominated the '40s and '50s. In the '70s, punks adopted the bomber for the military look while the '80s saw it make a mainstream comeback with wool collars and cuffs thanks to films like *Top Gun*, which reignited interest in the old-school military jacket. These days, the bomber isn't just reserved for blokes, with everyone from Alexander McQueen to Versace featuring bombers in their ready-to-wear collections.

1914

PENCIL SKIRT

Christian Dior showed a modern pencil skirt in his 1954 Autumn/Winter Collection in Paris. It was the first time Dior had moved away from 'The New Look', which he had fashioned in the late '40s, and began to adopt the fitted skirt style. His pencil skirt was figure-hugging and cut off just below the knee. Audrey Hepburn, Grace Kelly and Marilyn Monroe all helped raise the profile of the pencil skirt. It became a popular office-wear look and has since found a place in fashion beyond work wear, with Givenchy, Balmain and Roland Mouret all including variations of the skirt in their collections.

1954

UTILITY DRESS

Fabric was rationed in Britain in 1941, which limited the amount of new clothes people could make and buy, and in 1942 the government intervened in the mass production of high street fashions with the utility clothing scheme, which introduced new styles that complied with wartime rations. Designed to be affordable and durable, not fashionable, the 1940s utility dress was based on a military uniform and had the label 'CC41'. Despite the restrictions, women still found a way to make the wartime look somewhat more glamorous, often adding red lipstick and a turban or headband to their look. The utility dress was also usually paired with the iconic victory roll hairstyle, where the hair was styled into rolls that framed the face. The utility dress is still popular today, appearing in various modern takes from shirt to tie-waist dresses.

1942

HIGH-WAISTED BIKINI

High-waisted bikinis ruled women's beach style in the 1940s. One-piece swimsuits were still popular, but the high-waisted two-piece dominated this era, featuring figure-flattering control panels in the fabric over the stomach made from Lastex, and cups fitted inside the bra for a fuller shape. It would later be succeeded in popularity by a skimpier, navel-baring bikini, although girls with vintage style still wear the high-waisted bikini today.

1940s

FLAPPER DRESS

The Roaring Twenties introduced the world to the flapper, a woman who usually sported short hair, a shift dress that often resembled undergarments (and gave everyone a flat chest) and wore make-up and applied it in public – a scandalous manoeuvre in the post–World War I era. The flapper dress was usually short and often featured layers of fringing, and when women danced it swung up to reveal their underwear. This was a classic look of the Jazz Age, when women turned the table on the feminine fitted form in favour of looser cuts that represented comfort and liberation. It was a look that Coco Chanel helped create, which was dubbed 'garconne': a woman who rebelled against ladylike conventions.

1920s

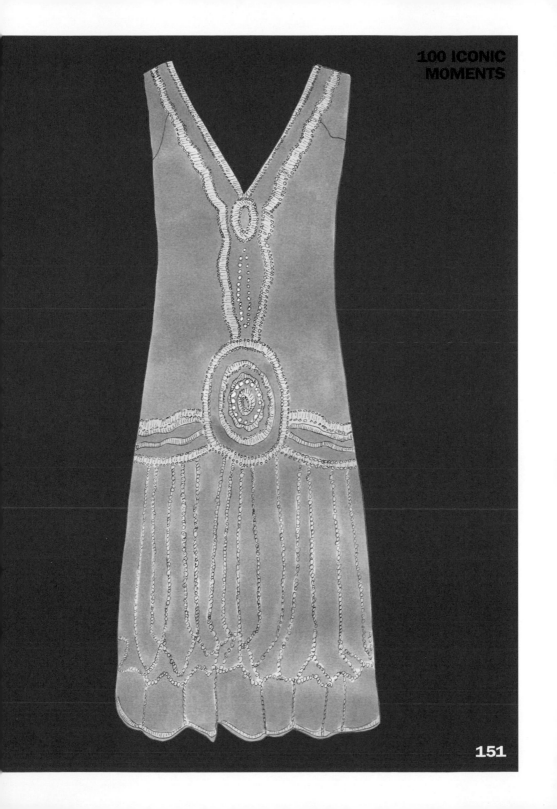

POODLE SKIRT

The poodle skirt came along in the '50s and was hailed as a fashion heroine in the rock 'n' roll scene. The skirt allowed the gal rockers to dance without restriction due to its wide-circle hem. Many of the skirts featured poodle appliqués – hence the name. The poodle was later replaced by flamingos and hot-rod cars. The skirt was first designed by Juli Lynne Charlot in the USA as a holiday-season skirt, but it became a hit with teenagers – as we can see in movies like *Grease*. The nostalgic silhouette is the ultimate symbol of 1950s Americana.

1950s

SLIP DRESS

The slip dress, complete with spaghetti straps, has become a late-20th century icon. The popular bias-cut silhouette might look like lingerie, but is designed to be worn as a dress. There were a few fashion designers who favoured this style, including John Galliano, who included a version in his Dior debut in 1996. One of his slip dresses was famously worn by Princess Diana in the same year. Calvin Klein and Narciso Rodriguez also embraced the sensual simplicity of the slip in the '90s – Rodriguez made a slip-style wedding dress for Carolyn Bessette who married John F. Kennedy Jr. in 1996. Nineties poster girls who made the slip dress red carpet famous include Gwyneth Paltrow, Kate Moss and Winona Ryder.

1990s

CROP TOP

The crop top became commonplace in the '80s
when it was mostly worn during aerobic exercise.
But it was Madonna who catapulted the crop top to
mainstream '80s fame when she wore one in the
Lucky Star video clip in 1984. The top first came
to the world's attention in the 1940s when it was
usually paired with a high-waisted skirt. By the '70s
it was more often worn with flared pants. The '80s
made it a pop culture staple and this continued
through to the '90s, when the crop got shorter
and sexier in the hands of Christina Aguilera and
Jennifer Lopez. Its enduring popularity continues
in fashion and runway shows today.

1980s

FAUX FUR COATS

Wearing fur isn't cool – just ask British fashion
designer Stella McCartney who has always been
at the forefront of the anti-fur debate. She prefers
faux fur when it comes to her runway collections,
and celebrities like Lily Allen have jumped on the
faux fur bandwagon. While faux fur was invented
in the 1910s, made out of synthetic fabric as a
cheaper alternative to real fur, it was McCartney
who made faux a fashion must. Other designers
who don't favour fur include Calvin Klein, Tommy
Hilfiger and Vivienne Westwood. *Vogue* editor
Anna Wintour, who often wears real fur, copped
a face full of custard pie in 2005 while on her
way to a Chloé show during Paris Fashion Week –
delivered on behalf of PETA (People for the Ethical
Treatment of Animals) protesters who don't support
Wintour's fancy for fur. Once perceived as a luxury
garment, fur might still occasionally find its way into
runway collections, but it's faux fur that's taking
its edgy place.

2000s

JUMPSUIT

The one-piece jumpsuit has long had a place in fashion, but never did it reign supreme like it did in the 1970s. Everyone from Elvis Presley to Suzi Quatro wore one – flamboyantly designed and often adorned with sequins, they were the perfect stage costume. After the '60s toyed with the jumpsuit and the '70s owned it, the one-piece made its way to the high street in the decades that followed. The '80s gave it a shoulder pad nudge, and the 2000s spawned the jumpsuit style affectionately known as 'the onesie'. But the jumpsuit actually dates back to 1919 when Ernesto Michahelles, an Italian artist of the Futurist movement, was the first to sew a one-piece garment that was designed to be easy to wear. These days, designers still repurpose the look, often with a nod to its '70s heyday.

1970s

100 ICONIC MOMENTS

ADORN-
MENTS

PANTYHOSE

American textile-company owner Allen Gant created the pantyhose in 1959, although they were known as sheer tights in the United Kingdom. The toe-to-waist stocking was usually made of nylon and spandex, which helped to tone flesh and make legs look longer and leaner; this was a welcome innovation in the era of rising hemlines. Over the decades pantyhose has changed – from fishnet varieties to flesh-toned sheers, control-top to toe-less varieties, it's found a way to exist in corporate life, evening events and cocktail hours.

1959

STILETTO HEELS

There's plenty of debate over who invented the stiletto heel, but it can be traced to Italian-born shoe designer André Perugia, who was working with fashion designer Pierre Poiret in Paris in the early 1900s. But the man who put the stiletto in fashion's high-end spotlight was Italy's Salvatore Ferragamo, who made his first pair for Marilyn Monroe in 1950. In those days the stiletto heel sat at just 3 centimetres in height (just over an inch), whereas today heels can tower up to 25 centimetres (around 10 inches). Stiletto heels are defined by the shape of the heel, which looks like the stem of a champagne glass, and not the height. They're designed to make a woman look taller, sexier and help her to embrace her inner female fatale. In the '80s, women were into corporate power dressing – the ideal place for a stiletto to thrive alongside boxy shoulder-pads and a two-piece suit.

1900s

AVIATOR SUNGLASSES

Described as pilot's glasses, the original Aviator
sunglasses were created in 1936 by optical
company Bausch + Lomb (who founded Ray-Ban).
Aviators became a well-known style in the '40s
when pilots used them while flying during World
War II, and in the '50s when Marlon Brando wore
them in the 1953 film The Wild One. The style
went mainstream in the '60s thanks to the movie
stars, like Brando, who embraced the glasses –
making those metal rims a hit with the masses.
The sunglasses had renewed fame in the '80s
when Tom Cruise and Val Kilmer made them iconic
in hit movie Top Gun. Over the years the lens colour
range has expanded, and now includes mirror,
tinted and pink-coloured lenses.

1936

PLATFORM SHOES

The platform shoe has a long history that dates
back to the Renaissance period, but it became
a fashion talking point in the 1930s because of
designers such as Salvatore Ferragamo. He was
inspired by *The Wizard of Oz* and created the
Rainbow platform sandal for Judy Garland in 1938.
It wasn't until the late '60s that the platform was
embraced by glam rockers like Marc Bolan of T-Rex,
and later KISS, and worn by teens and fashion
followers. The '70s saw the platform shoe make
a comeback thanks to fashion store and brand
Biba – its design fused '70s boho with the dawning
of '80s disco and was popular with both men
and women. In the '90s, girl group the Spice Girls
made a new type of platform shoe big: the platform
sneaker, which put a sneaker on top of a platform
heel. The shoe trend could be highly dangerous –
Vivienne Westwood put Naomi Campbell in a pair
of platform shoes in a 1993 show and Campbell
fell, making headlines. Lady Gaga is also a fan of
sky-high platform shoes.

1938

DESERT BOOTS

The desert boot was created by Nathan Clark of the Clarks shoes dynasty in 1949 and officially launched a year later. The iconic lace-up shoe is lightweight, made from suede, and it revolutionised footwear. Word has it Clark was inspired by British soldiers in Burma wearing a similar design in the late '40s. Everybody has rocked a pair of desert boots, including Bob Dylan, Steve McQueen, Liam Gallagher from Oasis and Florence Welch from Florence and the Machine. Even Sarah Jessica Parker has been seen purchasing a few pairs at a New York shoe shop. The design of the boot has remained relatively unchanged by Clarks since it was first released, and it has since been re-released in limited-edition runs by the brand.

1949

RAY-BAN WAYFARERS

Ray-Ban Wayfarers were designed at Bausch + Lomb (the same company who brought us Aviators) by Raymond Stegeman in the mid '50s. The story has it that the frame were specifically designed to be a classic. Wayfarers were a hit when they were released in the '50s, but their popularity waned throughout the '60s and '70s. It was punk-rock goddess Debbie Harry from NYC new-wave band Blondie who made the black frames an iconic fashion style once again. They truly became a rock 'n' roll staple when the frames went from metal to plastic (adopting a new plastic molding technology).

1956

CAMOUFLAGE

Camouflage conjures notions of war and military, and was originally designed to conceal soldiers and objects from enemies. The pattern was first used in World War I by the French military camoufleurs, who were a group of fine artists (usually cubist or impressionist painters) tasked with painting stationary objects with camouflage patterns. After the war, camouflage moved from combat to mainstream and fashion is still obsessed with the army-inspired pattern. The classic print in tan, browns and greens has been embraced by fashion designers who have found a place for it on t-shirts, denim, pants and dresses. Camouflage pattern has long been associated with countercultures like hip hop and the reggae and ska scenes.

1914

SHOULDER PADS

Shoulder pads were invented in 1877, originally built for footballers to protect their shoulders. They have since been used more for sartorial purposes, being deployed into a padded fabric that sits under jackets, dresses and blouses of women's clothing, peaking in fame in the '80s. But let it be known that it was Elsa Schiaparelli who first made shoulder pads fashion famous in the '30s, including them in her designs, which were often worn by film star Joan Crawford. By the late '30s shoulder pads became more masculine to fit with war times – think military references in women's jackets and coats – and even dress shoulders had a sturdier look. The humble shoulder pad still has a place in runway designs from the '90s to present day, always with a nod to its nostalgic past.

1877

CORSETS

By the 16th century, corsets were a staple fashion item. The undergarment had its origins in Italy and was worn by the likes of Catherine de Medici, a Florentine noblewoman who took the bodice-like structure to France when she married a French prince. Typically worn beneath garments, a corset makes the waist and torso appear smaller, flattening the breasts and emphasising the waist. The stiff undergarment remained a common feature in the 18th and 19th centuries, designed to define the midriff, support the back and improve posture while shaping the breast. Fast forward to the modern era and we can thank the Kardashian clan for reigniting the controversy surrounding the health risks that come with wearing corsetry, which is designed to slender the torso while tricking the waistline to obey the tummy-and-waist tuck – giving the concept of hourglass shape a whole new meaning.

1500s

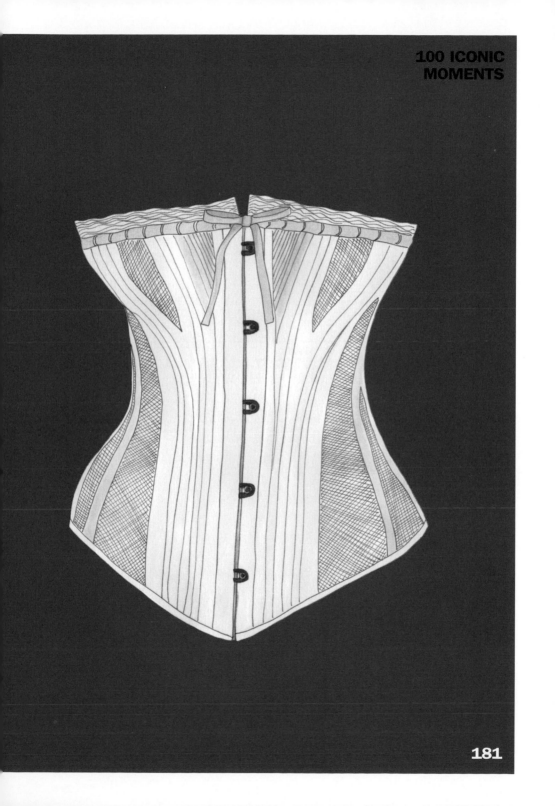

LEATHER FRINGING

Leather fringing appeared everywhere in the '70s, on suede jackets, leather jackets, shoes and handbags. The fringe had plenty of swing and when worn with platform shoes, flared pants and a '70s flick hairdo, the look was bohemian to the max. The hippie style was revitalised in 2016, with fashion designers like Ralph Lauren, Dolce and Gabbana and Proenza Schouler adopting elements of fringing in their collections – think fringe-tasselled bags, fringed strappy sandals and fringed skirt hemlines.

1970s

POLKA DOTS

Some say it was the gypsies and flamenco dancers who bought the polka dot print to the world in the 1860s, and it was certainly named after the popular polka dance from Bohemia, but the only print really took off when mid-19th century English dandies (fashionable men of the time) like Beau Brummell started wearing dotted scarves and bowties. After Beau was spotted wearing polka dots, ladies soon followed in his steps. The humble polka dot made modern headlines in the 1920s when Miss America winner Norma Smallwood was photographed wearing a polka-dot swimsuit, and by the 1930s, polka dots had found their way into Bakelite jewellery. Dior also used the bespeckled pattern in his 'The New Look' collection, while Marilyn Monroe famously wore a polka dot bikini in 1951. Walt Disney was inspired to create a polka-dot-loving mouse known as Minnie in the '60s and designers have continued to connect the fashion dots ever since.

1860s

FLAPPER HEADBANDS

Flappers were the cool fashion kids of the 1920s, and they loved the bob haircut; and what better accessory to keep the cropped style in place than bobby pins and a headband that sat across the forehead? Women of this era waved goodbye to long Edwardian locks in favour of shorter hairdos, like the bob or the shingle cut. These were designed to give the women of this era a more androgynous look, and the decorative flapper headband kept their hair in place while dancing; expensive head jewels added a feminine touch. The look was made famous by stars including silent film movie actress Louise Brooks and singer Josephine Baker.

1920s

CLOCHE HATS

The cloche hat was a cornerstone of the Jazz Age, a time when jazz music reigned and flappers ruled fashion. Invented in 1908 by Caroline Reboux, the hat was a popular look when teamed with the Eton crop haircut. The snug-fitting design was invented for comfort and worn closely fitted to the head like a cap. Cloche hats were predominantly made of felt in the early 1900s and later of straw and sisal. These hats were often adorned with jewels and brooches, scarves and feathers for a decorative emphasis.

1908

PERSOL 714S

Giuseppe Ratti founded eyewear company Persol – translating from Italian as 'for the sun' – in 1917 in Italy. He originally produced his sunglasses for aviators and athletes, and it wasn't until the mid '60s that the flexible sunglasses appeared in the USA. Actor Steve McQueen made the 714s famous – he wore them on set filming The Thomas Crown Affair and The Getaway, making them a cult must-have for men around the world. The Persol 714s continue to reign supreme in eyewear, and the classic design remains mostly unchanged except for a contemporary tweak.

1917

CAPES

A cape is a sleeveless outer garment that is part wrap and part coat, and is usually fastened around the neck. It's a convenient style that allows hands and arms to be free. The cape dates back to medieval times, but made its way into women's fashion in the 1850s when capes were widely used as evening wear, often trimmed with fur and designed to be worn over an evening dress. Paul Poiret was responsible for the cape's transformation into a modern fashion item, making the first tailored cape in muted tones with fur trims in 1911.

1850s

SADDLE SHOES

In the '50s, the cool kids danced the jitterbug and Lindy hop wearing saddle shoes. The footwear was a two-tone unisex shoe – similar to a bowling shoe – usually worn with bobby socks. Saddle shoes were adopted by high school students in the USA and were often worn with poodle skirts. While the footwear originated in the 1900s and were part of the gangster uniform in the '30s (think *The Great Gatsby*) it wasn't until the '50s that they became the shoe of choice for the trendy set. The shoes became iconic when movie stars started to wear them, and word has it women in the '50s wore them during the day while doing the chores – swapping into heels before their husbands got home from a day in the office.

1900s

CHANSONETTE BRAS

The Chansonette bra, a style originally released by underwear company Maidenform that became known as the bullet bra, was popular in the 1950s thanks to movie stars like Marilyn Monroe and pin-ups like Bettie Page. It was introduced in 1949 and had a cone-shaped cup stitched in a whirlpool pattern. The pointed bra didn't have any padding or wires and was designed to highlight the breast shape and exaggerate its form. It created the ultimate pin-up girl image, the cone-like contour of the breast part of the classic hourglass silhouette. Jean Paul Gaultier riffed off this style when creating his cone bra, which was immortalised by Madonna on her Blond Ambition tour.

1949

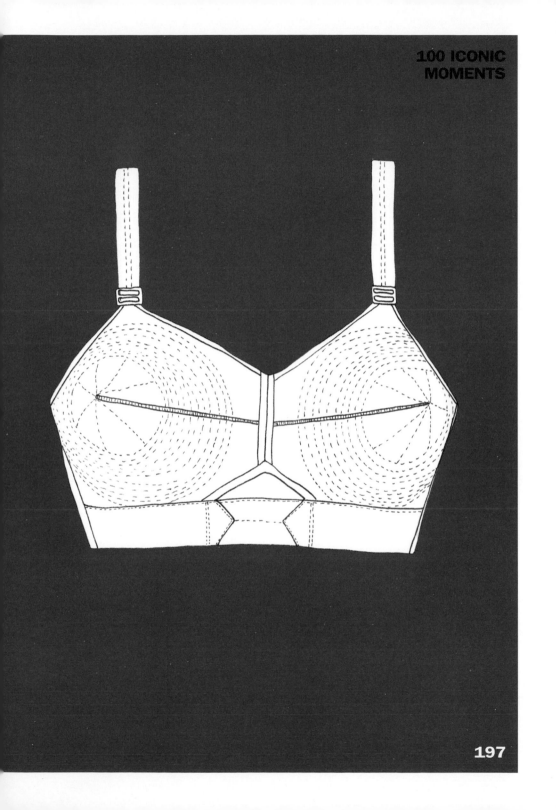

CAT-EYE SUNGLASSES

Cat-eye sunglasses ruled in the mid '50s. The glasses resembled cat eyes, with an upsweep design on the outer edges of the glasses where the arms joined the frame. It was Marilyn Monroe who helped steer the glasses to fame after she wore a pair in the film *How to Marry a Millionaire* in 1953. By the '60s cat-eye sunglasses were commonplace. Eyewear company Oliver Goldsmith designed an iconic pair of cat-eye sunglasses called the 'Manhattan', which Audrey Hepburn wore as part of her famous look in *Breakfast at Tiffany's*. Fashionable women often matched the cat-eye frames with a '60s beehive hairstyle (an iconic mod style where the hair is piled up in a cone-like shape and teased for height) – further catapulting their cool status.

1950s

GO-GO BOOTS

Go-go boots were designed by André Courrèges in 1964 and kick-started a trend for long boots. Courrèges was already known as one of the designers credited with inventing the miniskirt, and his go-go boots were calf-high plastic boots that got higher in length as the hemlines got shorter. Named after the French word 'la gogue' – which means happiness – the shoe became popular in the Swinging Sixties, particularly with the mod scene. Nancy Sinatra wore go-go boots on her Boots album cover, as did Jane Fonda in Barbarella, and Brigitte Bardot rocked the look in the late '60s in France.

1964

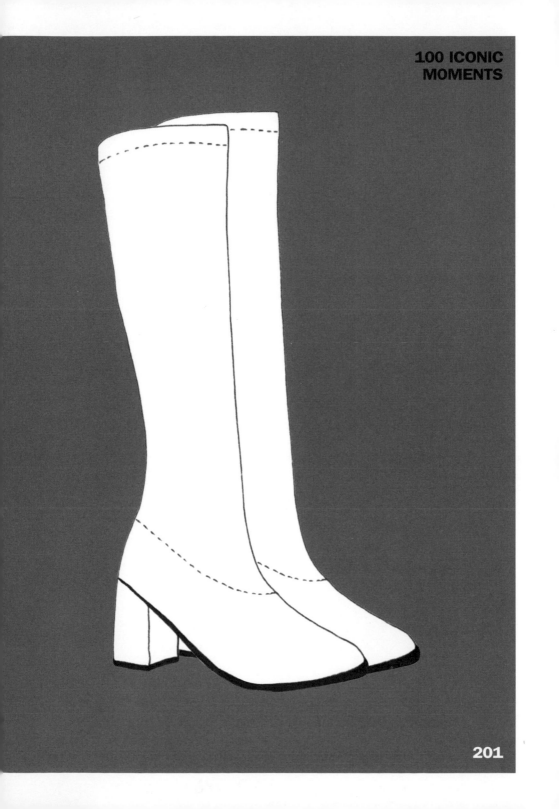

WIDE-BRIMMED HATS

The '70s belonged to the wide-brimmed floppy hat and Brigitte Bardot helped push it into the spotlight – often sporting a floppy hat while wearing a bikini. When her famous choucroute hair was topped with a floppy hat she embodied the essence of French chic. Young women wanting to mimic her bombshell look would simply add a hat.

1970s

PILLBOX HATS

First Lady of the United States of America
Jacqueline Kennedy first wore a pillbox hat in 1961.
The hat design had originated in the 1930s, when
milliners adapted the small brimless round hat for
its simple and elegant design, but the popularity
of the hat reached its peak in the '60s thanks to
Kennedy, who made it her trademark. On the day
her husband was assassinated in Dallas, Texas, in
1963, Jackie was wearing a Halston-designed pink
pillbox hat that matched her Chanel suit – it's an
image forever etched in history.

1963

PLAID

Plaid, or tartan as it was originally known, was worn by Scottish clans who used the fabric for heavy travelling cloaks designed to ward off the Scottish Highlands winter, and the patterns were distinct to each clan. Once plaid started being manufactured by the British and Americans and used in fashion in the '20s (when flannel shirts first reared their lumberjack head), it didn't take long until it was embraced by everyone from the punk scene to hipsters. The cross-hatched pattern was adored by designers from Vivienne Westwood to Alexander McQueen. In the '70s it was a symbol of rebellion, by the '80s counterculture had embraced it as a preppy stronghold (think St Elmo's Fire), and it was the fabric of choice for '90s grunge (think Singles).

1920s

PEARLS

Pearls were traditionally a luxury accessory worn by the rich and famous. It wasn't until the 1960s that pearls crossed over into the mainstream market via inexpensive plastic replicas, making the delights of a string of pearls available to all fashionable women. Pearls are perceived as a sign of respectability and women of note have always worn them, from Princess Diana, who favoured a pearl choker, to Angelina Jolie, who is often seen on the red carpet wearing pearls.

1960s

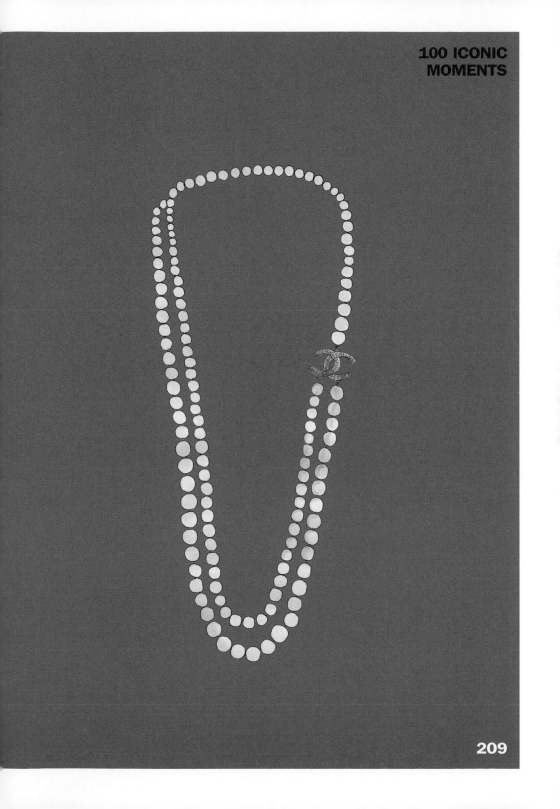

CHUCK TAYLORS

Converse All Stars lace-up sneakers were created in 1917 by Converse. American basketball player Charles 'Chuck' Taylor joined Converse as a sales guy (in the middle of his basketball career) and collaborated with the brand, helping to design aspects of the All Stars, and the shoes were eventually named after him in 1932. Chuck Taylors became a mainstay of sportswear before they infiltrated the leisurewear space. Embraced by everyone from athletes to musicians, they became particularly popular in punk and rock scenes, with New York's The Ramones and Nirvana wearing the rubber sole lace-up shoes as an act of pop culture rebellion. Nike bought the brand in 2003.

1917

OVERSIZED GLASSES

We have Jackie Kennedy Onassis and Marilyn
Monroe to thank for the popularity of oversized
sunglasses. Both women wore them religiously
in the '60s. Big frames continue to be worn by
celebrities who want to hide from paparazzi and
women who want to mimic the glam status cool.
The frames are generally made from bold black
plastic with oversized rims. sunglasses

1960s

BOATERS

The boater dates back to the 1880s, when the hat was first made in the English town of Luton in Bedfordshire. Boaters were also worn by gondoliers in Venice and they were apparently part of the FBI uniform pre–World War I. Traditionally made of straw, boaters were mostly worn by stylish men of status and influence. By the 1930s, its popularity eclipsed that of the trilby and Panama hat. It also became part of the school uniform of privileged school children. Now the humble boater is back and popular among female race-goers.

1880s

Smith
Street
Books

ISBN: 978-1-925418-32-3

CIP data is available from the National Library of Australia.

Publisher: Paul McNally

Project manager: Aisling Coughlan

Editor: Lauren Whybrow

Design concept: Michelle Mackintosh

Design layout: Heather Menzies, Studio31 Graphics

Illustrations: Juliet Sulejmani

Printed & bound in China by C&C Offset Printing Co., Ltd.

Book 28

10 9 8 7 6 5 4 3 2 1

For Sunny & Estelle

Jane Rocca